We, the people of the United States, in order to form a more perfect union, establish justice, insure domestic tranquility, provide for the common defense, promote the general welfare and secure the blessings of liberty to ourselves and our posterity, do ordain and establish this constitution for the United States of America.

Preamble to the U.S. Constitution, September 17, 1787

Report of the
National Commission
on the
Role and Future of
State Colleges and
Universities

To Secure the Blessings of Liberty

DISCARD

American Association
of State Colleges and Universities

© 1986 by
American Association of State Colleges and Universities
Washington, D.C.

Library of Congress Cataloging-in-Publication Data

American Association of State Colleges and Universities
National Commission on the Role and Future of State
Colleges and Universities.
To Secure the Blessings of Liberty.

1. State universities and colleges—United States. 2. Education,
Higher—United States—Aims and objectives. 3. Educational
equalization—United States. 4. Teachers—Training of—United
States. I. Title.
LB2329.5.A45 1986   378'.053   86-22338   ISBN   0-88044-080-5

Contents

Appendices

Foreword

by Allan W. Ostar and Stephen Horn

Establishment of the American Association of State Colleges and Universities (AASCU) on February 23, 1961, formalized the post-World War II emergence in the United States of a new type of public institution of higher learning: the comprehensive state college and university.

AASCU had its origins in the Association of Teacher Education Institutions (ATEI), founded in 1951. Nearly all of the original members of AASCU began as single-purpose institutions, most of them as normal schools. By 1950, all normal schools had become teachers colleges, and many of them were called state colleges or universities.

Prior to 1950, the activities and concerns of the teachers colleges had been confined largely to their respective states or, for a large number, to limited regions within their states. But with the rapid expansion of higher education enrollments following enactment of the GI Bill, the teachers colleges became the fastest-growing degree-granting institutions in the nation. As a result, their programs and services expanded and their horizons were greatly extended.

After ten years of coping with problems endemic to institutional expansion—the need for increased financial support, the impact of new curricula and a generation of ex-servicemembers on academic traditions, and the constant struggle for professional identity—ATEI members realized the urgency of creating a more broadly based national organization. What was required, they decided, was an association that recognized the development of comprehensive, multipurpose state colleges and universities as a growing, responsive, permanent presence on the nation's postsecondary landscape. Time, the dynamic American economy, and rapid social change had made the "single-purpose" public institutions virtually obsolete.

Thus it was, twenty-five years ago, that AASCU entered the scene as the "third force" in public higher education, a companion set of institutions with regional or statewide missions taking a seat at the national policy table alongside the National Association of State Universities and Land-Grant Colleges (NASULGC) and the American Association of Community and Junior Colleges (AACJC)—the three organizations that provide national leadership and coordination to America's public postsecondary system.

Today, there are more than 400 public institutions of higher learning that fit the "comprehensive state college and university" category, of which 372 are members of AASCU. Besides the former teachers colleges, the nucleus of the comprehensive institutions includes former technical institutes, agricultural schools, colleges open to women and minorities, mechanics institutes, YMCA or physical culture schools, and a significant number of former private, proprietary, or religious institutions later purchased by or given to the state. In addition, several AASCU-type institutions began as branches or off-campus centers of large public or private universities and others developed from the conversion of two-year junior colleges to four-year senior colleges.

Whatever their roots, the modern comprehensive state colleges and universities share the following characteristics: publicly established and controlled by state governance systems; primarily multipurpose institutions emphasizing both liberal and professional education; predominantly bachelor's and master's degree programs; emphasis on meeting diverse needs of different states and regions, primarily at the undergraduate and master's levels, but including less-than-four-year programs and doctoral programs in selected fields; primarily teaching institutions, with emerging chartered missions as centers of applied research and community service; predominantly open-access institutions that emphasize equal opportunity; and primarily funded from state taxes, with a tradition of low or moderate tuition charges. They serve upper, middle, and lower socio-economic class students and all regions of the country.

Over 2,500,000 students attended comprehensive state colleges or universities in 1985, more than one of every five in all of higher education. Nearly one-third of the bachelor's degrees, more than 27 percent of all master's degrees, and 5 percent of the doctorates earned in 1982 were awarded by state colleges and universities.

As liberal arts-based, professionally oriented institutions, the comprehensive state colleges and universities share the mission of: (1) liberal and practical education for the first job; (2) theoretical education to undergird the second, third, and succeeding careers; (3) education in personal and professional ethics so that career skills will be used appropriately; (4) continuing education in the humanities, sciences, and social sciences, so that each individual can use such knowledge to enhance his or her world understanding; and (5) support of a student's personal development and maturation. The values these institutions impart are basic: that education is an opportunity to better oneself as an individual; that education is an opportunity to better society through one's knowledge; and that all persons have a responsibility to all other persons.

As the needs of our nation and its people have changed significantly over the past quarter century, so, too, has American higher education. The expansion of knowledge has changed the form and structure of institutions. Expansion of the franchise and the concept of citizenship itself have brought new responsibilities to the nation's postsecondary institutions, both public and private.

Development of the comprehensive state colleges and universities has played an important part in expanding access to higher education, as President Truman's Commission on Higher Education foresaw in its 1947 Report, *Higher Education for American Democracy.* "Free and universal access to education, in terms of the interest, ability, and need of the student," that distinguished panel declared, "must be a major goal in American education."

The broadened access to higher education provided by comprehensive state colleges and universities over the past three decades has enabled the private liberal arts colleges to retain their small size and the large public land-grant/research universities to emphasize their research functions. Now, as AASCU enters its second quarter century, far-reaching changes in America's domestic and international environment challenge the comprehensive state colleges and universities to reexamine their role in service to the nation and to chart a new, revised course into the next century.

It was with precisely such a challenge in mind that the AASCU Board of Directors decided, in January 1985, to appoint a National Commission on the Role and Future of State Colleges and Universities. The Commission was asked to frame recommendations that could guide the universe of comprehensive state colleges and universities in responding to the dramatic changes occurring in our society, such as the growth in minority populations, accelerated obsolescence of job skills, increasing numbers of older and part-time students, expansion of regional economic development programs, the crisis in teacher education, and the need to add an international dimension to the undergraduate curriculum.

The Commission functioned as an independent body and prepared recommendations based on its own deliberations and the findings of four regional seminars conducted under Commission sponsorship during March and April 1986.

AASCU considers itself most fortunate and greatly honored that former Secretary of Education Terrel H. Bell accepted the invitation to chair the Commission, a decision that influenced twenty-one other distinguished Americans to participate in its work. Their recommendations—many of which are bold and imaginative—are addressed to state colleges and universities, to public policy makers, and to the general public. The Commission has met its challenge head on, leaving the next steps up to AASCU, its member presidents, faculties, trustees, administrators, alumni, governors, state legislators, the federal government, and the American people.

The work of the Commission has been generously supported by grants from the Andrew W. Mellon Foundation, the Exxon Education Foundation, and the John D. and Catherine T. MacArthur Foundation.

Allan W. Ostar is President of the American Association of State Colleges and Universities.

Stephen Horn, President, California State University, Long Beach, currently chairs the AASCU Board of Directors.

Letter of Transmittal

November 1, 1986

President Allan W. Ostar
American Association of State
  Colleges and Universities
Suite 700, One Dupont Circle
Washington, DC 20036

President Stephen Horn
California State University, Long Beach
Chairman of the Board of Directors
American Association of State
  Colleges and Universities

Dear Colleagues:

On behalf of the National Commission on the Role and Future of State Colleges and Universities, I am pleased to submit our Report, *To Secure the Blessings of Liberty*. All members of the Commission concur with the substance of the report and its recommendations.

The Commission would like to express its appreciation, first of all, to you and the other members of the AASCU Board of Directors for the opportunity to be of service to the Association and its member institutions. We hope that our Report will be of value to AASCU as it enters a second quarter century of leadership in the cause of public higher education.

We also wish to thank the members of the Commission's staff, their panel of Senior Advisors, and the participants in the four Commission-sponsored Regional Seminars, whose spirited discussions guided us in developing our Report. With respect to those Seminars, incidentally, the Commission believes that they represent a most fruitful approach to inter-institutional cooperation and policy formulation and recommends that AASCU give serious consideration to sponsoring such meetings on a continuing basis.

Lastly, we would like to thank the Andrew W. Mellon Foundation, the Exxon Education Foundation, and the John D. and Catherine T. MacArthur Foundation for the financial support that made our work possible.

On a personal basis, I would like to thank my fellow Commissioners for their time, their ideas, their collegiality, and their dedication to the task at hand. When we first assembled a year ago this month, I knew instantly that sharing this assignment with them would be a rewarding personal and professional experience—and I was right.

Sincerely,

Terrel H. Bell
Chair

1.

A Word to the American People

Ignorance is the enemy of democracy. Undeveloped intelligence that falls short of potential is a tragedy for the nation as well as a catastrophic denial of personal opportunity for the individual.

America has far too many people whose abilities are never awakened. This staggering waste and dissipation of our most precious resource means unemployment, unenlightened citizen participation or nonparticipation in elections and other processes of democracy, reduced productivity, and personal stagnation leading to frustration, crime, and abuse of freedom.

This wanton loss occurs because the nation is only partially committed to educating all of its people at a time when our international standing is being threatened and our economic future eroded by highly educated, highly motivated competitors abroad. For the sake of our future and in the interest of our humanity and civility, we must reorder our priorities to make a full and unequivocal commitment to learning.

Is it enlightened reason to take away access to higher education by making massive reductions in federal and state support of education? Under what rationale of priorities do we reduce student aid in the federal budget while increasing spending for the military? Ironically, the enormous cost of sophisticated and complex weapons that require skilled intelligence for utilization as well as advanced technological competence for production and maintenance dictates the very necessity for higher learning and more opportunity for education.

Our nation's economic future, our national security, and the education of our people are all tied together. This structure requires each of the elements of the triad as solid support. Weakening of one threatens the basic strength of the other two. That is why we must have an unprecedented commitment to education. Ignorance is not only costly—it is the passageway to a disastrous fall from which America may never recover. With a high school dropout rate ranging from 25 to 50 percent, and with almost 10 percent of our total population functionally illiterate, who can deny that we have a massive population of undereducated people? The United States is using up its intellectual capital but not replacing it. We must stop acting as though this state of affairs does not exist.

Public officials who propose budget reductions in education at a time when the republic is handicapped by the burden of an undereducated populace are unthinkingly abetting an act of national suicide. Their priorities are wrong. Their lack of insight and their misguided perceptions of the nation's needs contravene fundamental democratic values. They mock their countrymen who so desperately hope for a new era and the dawn of a learning society in America.

A Gathering Storm

The National Commission on the Role and Future of State Colleges and Universities sees a storm brewing in U.S. public higher education. Its turbulence will stir up questions about the role and future of state colleges and universities, presenting them with an unprecedented opportunity for answers that can place them in a position of national leadership.

This Report identifies some of the social, political, economic, and educational conditions that forecast the storm, and proposes a series of policy recommendations for governmental and educational leaders to help all Americans secure the blessings of liberty.

The storm warnings are unmistakable: our society is troubled, our economy endangered, our democratic values jeopardized, our international leadership threatened, our educational system embattled.

■ The nation's educational pipeline is contracting as the high school dropout rate mounts to over 25 percent, reaching levels as high as 45-50 percent for minorities in disadvantaged urban areas.

■ Black college students as a percentage of black high school graduates and Hispanic college students as a percentage of Hispanic high school graduates have declined annually since 1975.

■ By 1990, racial and ethnic minorities will account for 30 percent of all 18-22-year olds in the United States.

■ Despite gains in the early 1970s, at the end of the decade blacks still lagged behind whites in both attainment and achievement at each stage of education from high school through graduate and professional studies.

■ The education reform movements, while riveting public attention on the need to improve quality at both the elementary-secondary and the collegiate levels, have failed dismally to address the needs of minority youth, in many cases resulting in the uses of "excellence" and "quality" as code words for denial of access and opportunity to blacks, Hispanics, and other racial minorities.

■ In today's America, there are at least 23 million adults who have been identified as functional illiterates. In addition, some 13 percent of U.S. teen-agers, and up to 40 percent of minority adolescents, have been found to be functionally illiterate.

■ There are 50 million households in the United States where no family member holds a bachelor's degree—and the figure increases annually.

■ An American underclass is growing at an alarming rate; as many as one-fifth of the nation's children are living in poverty, and nearly half of poverty households are headed by single women.

■ There is an appalling increase in the frequency of adolescent pregnancies, perpetuating a poverty status for females with the greatest need for education but the greatest difficulty in obtaining it.

■ In an era of tight budgets, funds for postsecondary remedial education programs, including special counseling services needed for disadvantaged students, are being sharply curtailed.

■ As college costs have skyrocketed over the past ten years, including the cost of attending public institutions, federal student aid programs have failed to keep up, and have lost considerable ground in real dollars.

■ Across the land, the pendulum of reform in higher education is bringing new laws, policies, and regulations affecting the teaching profession, academic standards, admission and graduation requirements, testing practices, curricula, finance, student services, degree programs, administration procedures, governance, and institutional organization. This has meant that in many states, faculty members, administrators, and trustees at public colleges and universities have permitted their responsibilities for establishing admissions policies and academic standards to erode to the point where such policies are now being shaped in the political arena.

■ A nationwide shortage of elementary and secondary school teachers impends and will soon reach crisis proportions in some cities and states, with the profession needing over one million new teachers by the mid-1990s.

■ A dangerous imbalance in federal student aid programs exists between the percentage of federal support being channeled into grant or work-study programs and the percentage devoted to loans. Whereas in 1980 some 65 percent of federal student aid was in the form of grants or work-study programs, with 35 percent in loans, today that ratio has been reversed, with 65 percent of federal support in loan programs. This means that thousands of college and university graduates are entering the world of work already saddled with huge debts in the America of the late 1980s.

■ An Education Commission of the States (ECS) report found that in 1985 the number of 14-24-year olds who compose America's entry-level labor pool is shrinking, while at the same time "the number of young people who are disconnecting from school, work and the benefits they confer is on the rise." Consequently, poorly motivated teen-agers, lacking fundamental literacy skills and unacquainted with the responsibilities and demands of the work world, are "at risk of never living up to their potential, never leading productive adult lives."

■ Recent studies reveal that American college students, compared with their peers overseas, are poorly informed on global issues and lack an understanding of their country's role in international affairs.

A ''Marshall Plan'' for the States

These storm signals bode ill for the quality of American life. Nothing short of a creative state-by-state effort to strengthen education at all levels, comparable to the Marshall Plan in scope, cost, and dedication, can ensure the preservation of our democratic legacy for the twenty-first century.

■ indicates a Commission recommendation

In the judgment of the Commission, the dimensions of such an effort require that:

- At least 35 percent of American adults should have a college degree by the year 2001.
- State colleges and universities must assume the leadership role in producing the one million additional public school teachers required to meet the needs of elementary and secondary education during the next decade.
- State colleges and universities should direct their academic resources and institutional priorities toward working cooperatively with public schools and community colleges to reduce the high school dropout rate by 50 percent over a ten-year period.

In this Report, the Commission seeks to delineate the role state colleges and universities—a U.S. resource of immeasurable value—must play in that nationwide effort and what public leaders must do to help those institutions fulfill their role as stewards of higher learning.

The Commission has prepared its Report, therefore, as an essentially *political* document—political, in the broad sense that it is addressed to the body politic, both outside and within the higher education community.

The Report is intended for anyone concerned with public policies affecting state colleges and universities. And in contemporary America, that ought to mean everyone, for these are our nation's mainstream campuses—the institutions that should be equipped to offer everyone who wants to earn a bachelor's degree the opportunity to do so.

State colleges and universities today form the centerpiece of the U.S. public higher education system. Chartered to serve the regions and the states in which they are located, positioned between the community colleges and the land-grant/research universities, the state colleges and universities have a pivotal, continuing role as primarily teaching institutions and an emerging mission as centers for basic and applied research and community service. Their continued growth and vitality depend on enlightened academic, fiscal, governance, and management policies developed cooperatively by political and educational leaders committed to the concept that education represents a state's wisest investment in its future.

A major test of the viability of those policies and the effectiveness of that leadership lies just ahead as public higher education faces the complex of social, economic, technological, and demographic changes that are dramatically reshaping American society and profoundly affecting the U.S. role in world affairs.

The Commission perceives these structural changes in our national life as an unprecedented opportunity for state colleges and universities—a test of their resilience and their ability to respond in new and daring ways to challenges to fundamental democratic values, to the imperatives of broadening access to higher education while sustaining program quality, to the urgent needs of business and industry in the realm of economic development, and to the stark facts of international life as an interdependent world prepares to enter yet another dangerous century. All of these challenges will require educational and political leadership of the highest order, with public policies fashioned for the years 2001 and beyond, to build a republic of learners.

2.

Regarding Public Higher Education and Democratic Values

Religion, morality, and knowledge, being necessary to good government and the happiness of mankind, schools and the means of education shall forever be encouraged.

Article Three, The Northwest Ordinance, July 1787

Democracy depends on the informed consent of the governed. Because experience has taught us that being informed cannot be left to chance, schooling and education have been a focus of attention in the United States from the inception of the republic 200 years ago.

Historically, under the Tenth Amendment to the Constitution, public responsibility for the support and control of education is vested in the states, which have been the basic source of laws and charters granted to postsecondary institutions during the past two centuries. In the nation's earliest times, to be a college graduate was to be a part of an elite group. It meant that person was either rich or bright. As the decades went by, the United States came to realize that a small, educated elite was not consistent with its democratic goals, so public policies were developed to break down the barriers to educational opportunity.

After establishment of the public normal schools in Massachusetts in the late 1830s, as America's frontier pushed westward, the early territorial legislatures provided for free public colleges that would be equally open to all—a concept that received great impetus from the passage of the Land-Grant Act of 1862.

With its emphasis on equity and opportunity at all levels, America's public system of education has enriched our society in every conceivable way.

Educated people bring social and economic benefits to the communities and states in which they live. They have learned how to become productive citizens and active, responsible participants in their country's affairs.

Over and over, public schools and colleges have proved to be the wellspring of democracy. In modern times, the GI Bill, the National Defense Education Act of 1958, the Supreme Court's *Brown v. Board of Education* decision, the Higher Education Act of 1965, and its subsequent amendments all attest to that fact. Since 1960, an expanded system of comprehensive state colleges and universities and community colleges has extended educational access to millions who were previously barred from postsecondary education either because of stringent restrictions or because they could not afford it. Recently, these institutions have designed nontraditional programs addressing the learning needs of people where they are—in the work place, including active military service—in terms of their own educational development.

Most Americans view education as a national investment in the preservation and strengthening of social values. Since the time of Thomas Jefferson, our political and governmental system has been predicated on an informed citizenry. "I know of no safe depository of the ultimate powers of the society but the people themselves," Jefferson wrote in 1821, "and if we think them not enlightened enough to exercise their control with a wholesome discretion, the remedy is not to take it from them, but to inform their discretion by education." Between now and the century ahead, our citizens will have to make sophisticated and enlightened judgments about complex scientific, technical, and moral issues, ranging from the international implications of acid rain to the development of nuclear arms.

Access, Equity, Opportunity

Comprehensive state colleges and universities were developed to make higher education *accessible* to all who seek to continue their education; *affordable*, to put a chance to go to college within everyone's reach; and *accountable* to the states and communities that support them.

But state colleges and universities today face a serious dilemma. Just as the concepts of *equity* and *opportunity* were reinforced by public laws and policies, the current efforts to improve the nation's educational system are guided by an emphasis on the need for *quality* and *excellence*. Therefore, policy makers must face the question of how to reconcile the divergent forces that may be perceived to exist between the goals of excellence and quality, on the one hand, and the goals of equity and opportunity, on the other.

Without quality in education, the nation loses its strength. Without equity in education, democracy ceases to function. The Commission believes that ways must be found to manage the excellence/equity equation so that the boundaries of our public higher education system are extended, not limited.

It is not necessary to give up the goal of educational opportunity in order to achieve excellence. It is not a case of either-or, but both: "True educational excellence in our democracy," the Trustees of the Educational Testing Service have declared, "is not possible without true educational equity."

The "Low Tuition Principle"

One means of safeguarding and expanding access to postsecondary education in the public sector is to keep tuition at state colleges and universities as low as possible, a principle that has undergirded the development of public higher education from earliest times. According to the low-tuition principle, although costs vary from state to state, tuition levels in the public sector should encourage, rather than deny, access to postsecondary education. The principle is based on the concept that society recognizes the fundamental values inherent in education and that national survival depends on the nourishment of those values. Accordingly, society should bear a significant part of the financial cost of a student's college education.

The parental generation pays, primarily through state and federal taxes, for the education of the younger generation who attend public postsecondary institutions. Then, members of the younger generation, as college graduates, enter the work force, earn income, quickly become taxpayers, and in their productive years pay, in turn, for the public higher education of members of the next generation.

Society's investment in education is thus constantly renewed: by paying taxes, each generation accepts the responsibility to increase educational opportunity for successive generations. The Commission views the low-tuition principle in higher education as an extension of the free public elementary and secondary school system, an extension that becomes all the more necessary as America's technological and social complexity increases, confronting society and education with new problems.

Several of these problems are highlighted by current demographic data showing that the highest birth rate, the lowest high school graduation rate, the lowest rate of participation in higher education, and the highest incarceration rate all describe a single subset of the U.S. population—the growing underclass. Furthermore, the data on the nation's more advantaged populations indicate that the traditional family structure of just two decades ago is changing drastically, including vastly increased numbers of women in the work force, posing dislocations of traditional values and adding to the nation's dilemma.

The Commission recommends that, in formulating long-range plans for public higher education, state policy makers strive to keep tuition levels at state colleges and universities as low as possible, and that faculty members, administrators, and trustees at those institutions incorporate a commitment to ''the low-tuition principle'' in policies relating to institutional accessibility.

Low tuition levels require appropriation of state tax funds sufficient to attract and retain highly qualified faculty members, purchase up-to-date equipment, utilize modern instructional technology, and otherwise ensure that requirements for maintaining academic quality are met.

Higher Education and Public Service

U.S. higher education has a long history of preparing young adults for responsible civic leadership. However, in recent years, with the nation's problems becoming more complex, social scientists and other educators have observed that the interest of college students in their obligations as citizens appears to have diminished. More and more of them, studies show, are preoccupied with personal goals and career aspirations, with such preoccupations being reinforced by curricula that overstress vocationalism and understress the responsibilities of citizenship in a democracy.

To counter this trend, a number of public and private colleges and universities have begun to provide students with the opportunities to participate in public and community service activities as part of their undergraduate experience. Institutional encouragement of students to take advantage of such opportunities benefits society as a whole by extending education, by inducing individual participation in the political process, and by enhancing student understanding of the general welfare.

"Public and community service," the Education Commission of the States (ECS) has reported, "can do more than any academic seminar to counter provincialism and imbue [in students] a sense of responsibility to others."

The social and educational value of public and community service, in the Commission's judgment, is clear. It is a concept that should form the nucleus of the general education component of a student's learning experience, a value basic to enlightened citizenship. The Commission recommends, therefore, that state colleges and universities recognize the value of student participation in public and community service activities and make every effort to integrate public and community service into the undergraduate curriculum.

3.

Regarding Educational Opportunity in the United States

In these days, it is doubtful that any child may reasonably be expected to succeed in life if he is denied the opportunity of an education. Such an opportunity, where the state has undertaken to provide it, is a right which must be made available on equal terms.

The Supreme Court of the United States, in *Brown v. Board of Education*, 1954

In a society in which knowledge is a source of wealth, deprivation of access to higher education is a form of bondage. The social, economic, political, and cultural complexity of contemporary America requires a much higher level of education for everyone than ever before envisioned. Entry level jobs in the increasingly technical service economy require advanced levels of knowledge and skills. Yet only 19 percent of adults over twenty-five in this country have a bachelor's degree.

Only 8.8 percent of black Americans, 7.8 percent of Hispanic Americans, and less than 1.5 percent of Native Americans have a bachelor's degree. Nearly 50 million American families have never had a college graduate in their households. While minority communities are the most rapidly growing segment of our population, their rates of participation in higher education, except for Asian Americans, are actually declining.

To arrest this dangerous trend, we must ensure that all individuals who aspire to earn a bachelor's degree have the opportunity to attempt to fulfill that aspiration. Indeed, in order for the United States to maintain a leadership position in the world, and for its faltering economy to regain its strength in the face of international competition, at least 35 percent of American adults should have a college degree by the year 2001.

To accept this challenge, state colleges and universities will have to embark on an educational venture without precedent. Over the next ten years, these institutions will have major responsibility to produce one million public school teachers capable of working with the most diverse group of students ever to enter America's schools. The state colleges and universities will have to direct their academic resources and efforts toward working with the public schools and the community colleges to cut the high school dropout rate in half by 1996. Only by deliberately reaching out into the elementary and secondary schools and helping to salvage those students who might otherwise drop out will the nation be able to produce the numbers of college-educated people needed for the next century.

Responding to this challenge requires acknowledgment and acceptance: (a) by faculty members, of the necessity to become more skilled and adept in the assessment of student learning and progress; (b) by legislators and institutional leaders, of the imperative to respond effectively to the diverse educational needs of the nation's rapidly growing populations—minorities and new immigrants; (c) by public policy makers and college administrators, of the need to maintain educational support programs, often called remedial education, to overcome handicaps of earlier academic preparation that may have been weak or inadequate; (d) by the nation as a whole, of the need to produce multilingual citizens for a multilingual society and interdependent world; (e) by public officials, of the great national asset represented by the number and diversity of state colleges and universities.

One Million Teachers

Nowhere is there a greater need for leadership in higher education than in the preparation of teachers for the nation's public schools. The rapidly changing demographic structure of our society is creating serious shortages of teachers at all levels from early childhood education through the high school disciplines. Bilingual and multilingual teachers have been recruited in Europe, for example, to fill this year's positions in American schools.

Just to keep the doors of the public schools open, this country will need one million new elementary and secondary teachers, educational specialists, and school administrators to be trained and placed over the next ten years. With their historic roots as teacher education institutions, America's state colleges and universities are the sector of higher education with the primary responsibility and capacity for meeting this need.

Working in close cooperation with the public schools and teacher organizations, state colleges and universities must:

■ ensure that the academic preparation of teachers meets the highest standards expected by the schools and by the public;

■ attract more talented students, including greater numbers of minority students, into the teaching profession;

■ work in collaboration with teachers in the classrooms at all levels to solve practical problems of improving their teaching skills, developing better methods of student assessment, developing more effective curricula, and enhancing student motivation for learning.

This commitment cannot be made or fulfilled by schools or colleges of education alone. It must be made by all departments and disciplines and reinforced at the top levels of institutional leadership. Every faculty member should be held responsible for making a contribution to raising the level and quality of public education to meet the needs of the next century.

Because the crisis in teacher education is national in scope, the Commission recommends that Congress reinstitute the student loan forgiveness program for college graduates entering the teaching profession.

Frontiers in Facilitating and Assessing Student Learning

Recent criticisms of higher education have centered on the weaknesses in generic skills that many college graduates reveal. Some state colleges and universities have raised their entrance standards to ensure that all students will perform at a predetermined level, and most rely on traditional course tests and nationally standardized examinations to chart student progress. These approaches to assessment mask the need to search continuously for pedagogical techniques that facilitate learning. Such approaches also exclude many capable students from the opportunity to achieve an education.

State colleges and universities should be in the forefront of the movement to develop more effective methods of assessing the educational progress of students.

Assessment should be seen primarily as a means of enhancing the effectiveness of educational programs, not just as a means of demonstrating academic quality.

Because the Commission is convinced that much of vital importance has yet to be learned and understood about the instructional value of assessment and its use, it recommends that state college and university faculties assign high priority to research on pedagogy at all levels; develop coherent plans for determining when, where, and to what extent each student should demonstrate progress toward an agreed-upon set of bachelor's degree-level skills; and, paralleling such measures, design instructional strategies to correct deficiencies and to assist students to achieve at higher levels.

Institutional Diversity

Responding to the challenges inherent in meeting different needs and developing diverse talents cannot be accomplished by a monolithic design of higher education. Similarly, no single institution can be expected to offer the complete variety of courses that would permit it to respond to every challenge. It should not be surprising, therefore, that American higher education is by any yardstick the most diversified in the world. Its institutions are large and small, urban and rural, public and private, two-year, four-year, graduate, and professional. They may emphasize graduate and research programs, undergraduate teaching, or cooperative programs with industry. Their students may be historically or predominantly from minority groups. The foregoing characteristics combine in various ways at institutions having two-year or four-year degree programs that range from primarily technical to broad and comprehensive curricula.

State colleges and universities are characterized by diversity. Even when two such institutions may at first glance appear similar, significant differences emerge—between their special curricula (for example, Canadian Studies versus Afghan Studies, or pure mathematics versus mathematics education); their student body (residential versus commuting); purely undergraduate versus graduate; or the socioeconomic compositions of their campuses. In this fashion each state strives within its own higher education governance framework to provide and ensure maximum educational opportunity for its citizens. It is essential, therefore, that every effort be made to maintain such distinctions among institutions and their curricular and instructional programs. Maintaining diversity results in the cultural and economic enrichment of the communities and regions the institutions are chartered to serve.

Within the context of institutional diversity, special attention is due the significant role the thirty-four public historically black institutions have played and are expected to play. Established at a time when no other higher educational opportunities were available to the vast majority of black students, they have helped this country benefit from the development of talents among black Americans. They have done so under the most adverse conditions and in ways bordering on the miraculous. They have had to function in a manner that embodies the essential merits of access and opportunity.

Because our society still needs much progress before black young people of traditional college age can find at any campus of their choice an environment conducive to their educational and personal development, the historically black institutions will continue to occupy an important niche among higher education institutions in serving their historical clientele.

Enrolling approximately 27 percent of all black students in public four-year institutions, the historically black public institutions today must be regarded as playing an expanded role in public postsecondary education. They must be recognized as having the same kind of regional significance in regard to applied research and community service that pertains to any other state college or university. Their experiences have made them reservoirs of skills and understanding for teaching and nurturing underprepared students. They have at the same time moved into the mainstream of higher education, as evidenced by the proportions of their graduates who have proceeded to earn doctoral degrees. They possess a rich heritage which, through proper recognition and support, will continue to strengthen and increase access to higher education.

Remedial Education

Remedial education is not new to American higher education and has existed since 1636. Colleges have provided it for every wave of immigration and for every new group of students for 350 years. Freshman composition programs, for example, have always included, at least in part, remedial spelling, grammar, and rhetorical instruction. Compensatory efforts have long been made to overcome the lack of certain mathematical skills. Such efforts have been accepted without indictments, given the large differences in the levels of development of school districts around the country, and have greatly helped to ensure graduation by those admitted to college.

Now, as society becomes ever more diverse, the number and type of educational disparities have increased, and with them, the increasing need for appropriate remedial programs. Recently immigrated students, for example, while they may be fully qualified for higher education, must continue to become proficient in the English language while pursuing their studies. Students from inadequate rural or inner-city high schools may be deficient in oral communications skills. Students talented in the arts may need help in mastering the sciences. Almost all students need specific assistance in written expression. But these deficiencies ought not to be permitted to destroy a student's opportunity to pursue a higher education.

For the foreseeable future, state colleges and universities must plan to provide remedial instruction. Recognizing that the foundation of college persistence and achievement is solid academic preparation in high school, state colleges and universities should make a concentrated effort to reduce the incidence of postsecondary remedial education by becoming more actively and directly involved in the preparation of high school students for college study.

More school/college cooperative programs should be developed that not only stimulate the talented, but also guide, enrich, and raise the performance levels of underperforming students. This process ought to include joint meetings of college and high school faculty members and administrators and a sharing of data on student performance.

Financing Opportunity for All

Basic to our country's approach to education is the pivotal idea that the blessings of liberty should not be dependent on social class. It is, indeed, a moral tenet in America that a class-based society is wrong. One of the goals of the concept of universal education that has guided the development of public elementary, secondary, and higher education systems is to equip each individual to "break out" of underclass status—to "be all that you can be." If educational opportunity is stifled, if the chance to go to college is placed beyond the reach of large numbers of high school graduates, we will produce an elitist system of higher education—the very danger the state colleges and universities were created to guard against.

The GI Bill affirmed the tremendous dividend the American people could earn on their investment in expanding educational opportunities. Then, beginning with the Eisenhower Administration, the nation achieved political consensus on establishment of a federal student financial aid program to enable more students to go to college, so that qualified men and women who wanted to continue their education beyond high school, but who could not afford to do so, would not be denied that opportunity.

Over the years, spanning the presidencies of Kennedy, Johnson, Nixon, Ford, and Carter, such federal aid took the form of Pell Grants, loans, and work-study programs, and the resultant investment in America's economic future has grown. Our economy has been strengthened, our security safeguarded, and our society nourished. Students from families in all walks of life have benefited from that financial aid program. *Seventy-five percent* of all student aid available in U.S. colleges and universities today, in both the public and private sectors, is *federal aid*.

Tragically for the American people, the federal student financial aid program today is on the chopping block in Washington. In 1981, the value of the federal student assistance program was challenged by the new Administration, which began to recommend deep cutbacks in the annual congressional appropriations supporting it. So effective has been that challenge that in the last five years federal student financial assistance purchasing power was cut by 25 percent.

The current Administration, in other words, seeks to cut student financial aid in order to help reduce the deficit. But increases in student aid have *not* added to the deficit. In fact, from 1980 to 1986 the federal deficit *doubled* in constant dollars while federal expenditures for education at all levels *declined* by 16 percent.

In addition, because of increases in college tuition, the percentage of federal student aid awarded as grants has declined, while reliance on student loans has grown, to the point where college graduates today are burdened with debts in excess of $10,000 before they enter the work place. The nation has embarked on an indentured student policy to finance higher education.

Congress should take steps to provide sufficient funds for student financial assistance to rectify the existing imbalance in the federal financial aid program so that the amount of assistance channeled into grants and work-study would be at least equal to that appropriated for student loans.

Our national investment in higher education is not part of the deficit problem. Instead, it is part of the *solution*. An educated populace is a productive populace, earning and returning a portion of that earning power to society in the form of taxes. Education is not a luxury; we cannot be strong either militarily or economically unless we are also strong educationally.

Public policy makers will know that all individuals who aspire to earn a bachelor's degree shall have gained the opportunity to do so, when: (1) cost is not a barrier; (2) minorities are participating in and completing higher education at rates that match their proportions in the population; (3) substantial attention is given to eliminating limitations of access for those having physical disabilities; and (4) adult learners, and particularly single parents, find no roadblocks based on age or gender hindering their access to higher education.

4.

Regarding Higher Education and Economic Development

Our nation's universities and schools have a vital role to play in revitalizing America's competitiveness. . . .Without strong educational institutions, the United States will not be able to capitalize on our key potential strengths in technology and human resources.

The President's Commission on Industrial Competitiveness, January 1985

Historically, America's economic growth—and thus its national security—has been inextricably linked to the development of human resources and the applications of advances in research and technology to every sector of the nation's business and industry. The greatest threat to the future security and well-being of our nation is the waste of human beings through their inadequate education. Our country must chart a path toward excellence, with policies that encourage all individuals to perform at the peak of their abilities, or risk becoming economically subordinate to those countries willing to do so.

The map of every state is dotted with economic backwaters where educational levels are low, unemployment is high, and prospects for growth are dim. State and local leaders know that such communities, whether rural or urban, will never attract new economic activity unless these conditions are turned around. Recent studies show that in a business' decision to relocate, such factors as the quality of the public schools, local higher education and cultural centers, and communications facilities, are often as important as access to raw materials, markets, or cheap labor.

State colleges and universities have a vital role to play, both in improving the quality of public education in their respective states and regions, and in stimulating the business climate through the application of knowledge resources to business problems.

Investment in Human Capital

Experience and common sense tell us that educated people:
- bring economic benefits to their communities and states,
- get better jobs,
- earn higher wages,
- pay more taxes,
- stimulate America's cultural, intellectual, and scientific progress,
- and become more productive and responsible citizens.

Today's state colleges and universities are the generators of the service economy, training professionals in business, computer science, engineering, health, teaching, and other service sectors with growing needs for well-educated personnel. By providing access to professional careers for the broadest cross-section of Americans, including women and members of minority and immigrant groups, public colleges and universities represent a pathway into the American mainstream for individuals and families who would otherwise not have the opportunity to make this step, thus helping to ensure the stability of our free economy and our democratic government.

Policy makers should do all in their power to keep the college doors open, both literally and figuratively. Closing the doors of a college or university devalues the state's human capital portfolio and removes its resources from those available for investment in future economic growth—a shortsighted solution to a long-term problem.

When a decision is reached to close a state college or university, such action should be taken only as a last resort—only if the state is certain that its educational investment is being reinvested elsewhere, and only if access to higher education opportunities is not being foreclosed.

Partners in Regional Economic Development

State colleges and universities link the country in a network of knowledge available for application to problems of regional economic development. They help governments and industries find new uses for old resources to make a region's economy more secure.

A recent study by SRI International provides myriad examples of the positive impact colleges and universities have on the economy of their regions, expanding human capital through education and training, generating new technologies, new products, and new services through basic and applied research, and helping businesses maintain their competitive edge by sharing knowledge resources and transferring innovations from sector to sector throughout our economy.

State governments should examine the role that public higher education can play in regional economic development, including the possible expansion of institutional responsibilities in the areas of research and public service.

Higher education institutions, both public and private, can and should help governments and businesses achieve economic development goals through:

■ Economic Research and Analysis, including gathering and housing regional economic data, and assisting governments and business with data analysis,

■ Technical Assistance, through faculty consulting or centers organized to assist businesses to increase their competitiveness,

■ Research and Development, including cooperative research with business and industry,

■ Technology Transfer, applying knowledge, expertise, and technological developments to new sectors of the economy,

■ New Business Development, including business incubators, and university entrepreneurship that stimulates local business.

But efforts by individual institutions and the states alone will not ensure that our country's economy will be internationally competitive. Congress should create a national program to enhance the role of colleges and universities in community service and economic development. Such a program should encourage the involvement of higher education institutions with government, labor, business, and industry in planning, research, and development activities that promote expansion and retention of jobs and foster linkages that contribute to regional, state, and national economic growth.

Adult and Continuing Education

There is little need to search beyond the fact of the increasing average age of those who enroll in college to be convinced that state colleges and universities must address the educational requirements of individuals older than twenty-five. New careers, more effective participation by citizens, continued intellectual vitality, single parenthood, women reentering the work force, expansion of leisure activities—all have been noted as sources of the increase in college participation by adults.

Economic shifts, plant closings, and depressions in the local economy create a particularly poignant need to which public colleges and universities can respond through retraining adult workers for new occupations or upgrading their skills to improve productivity.

In order to respond to these needs, state colleges and universities should restructure their modes of delivery of instruction and services to give adult and part-time students full access to undergraduate and graduate programs. Specifically, institutions committed to serving adult learners should build on tested cooperative models: work-study programs, instructional television, instruction at the work place, and faculty-designed computer-aided instruction.

Access to continuing education programs should be provided in all regions of the states, to give working people the chance to pursue job advancement while fulfilling their civic and family responsibilities.

To ensure that working adults have meaningful access to such programs, the federal government should extend financial aid on a full-parity basis to all part-time and adult students.

Research

Research as a process of rational and creative inquiry leads to new ideas, concepts, understandings, and products. Because successful, high-quality research depends at its core on the developed skills of critical thinking and reasoning through analysis and synthesis, it is both an integral part and an outcome of higher education.

There has long been an underestimation of the place of both basic and applied research at state colleges and universities. People are often surprised to learn that research at state colleges and universities has resulted in breakthroughs in such areas as robotics, artificial intelligence, and biotechnology, in addition to the excellent social science and historical research and creative scholarly activity focused on the states and communities they serve. The talents among the faculty and students at these institutions have been underestimated and, therefore, underutilized. Over time, however, state colleges and universities have expanded the array of people who have the ability not only to do research themselves but also to teach research skills.

The contributions that can be made by state colleges and universities to the economic development of their regions, as well as the state and the nation at large, depend on the extent to which business and government can capitalize on the knowledge and achievements of their faculties through research, as well as teaching and service.

In the future, comprehensive state colleges and universities can be expected to continue to be involved in innovative research without becoming replicas of the research universities.

Research programs at state colleges and universities should continue to be developed, not only to meet the increasing needs of business and industry, but also to enhance state and regional information resources and to improve the quality of life. Such programs promote private-sector employment by developing a region's natural resources in an environmentally sound manner, while at the same time adapting new technologies to a region's specific economic needs.

5.

Regarding American Higher Education in an Interdependent World

No child should grow to adulthood in America without realizing the promise and the peril of the world beyond our borders. Progress made in teaching about world affairs must not lag behind progress made in other areas of American education.

President Lyndon Johnson's Message to Congress accompanying the International Education Act, 1966

In 1984-85, U.S. higher education was the object of three major critiques examining the state of affairs on the nation's campuses, ranging from the quality of instruction through the performance of students to the scope of the curriculum. Although the reports from the National Endowment for the Humanities, the Association of American Colleges, and the National Institute of Education varied in emphasis, their principal message was essentially the same:

America's colleges and universities have become too utilitarian, too vocational in their orientation, too parochial in their world outlook, with their curricula incoherent and in a state of disarray. Campuses have become "supermarkets," the critics charged, with narrow specialties the order of the day and the humanities on the decline.

Perhaps most alarming were the warnings in all three studies that American college students in the closing years of the twentieth century are seriously deficient in their knowledge of world affairs and their country's role in the international scene. Many colleges and universities in both the public and private sectors were found to be woefully inadequate in giving students an opportunity to study the languages and cultures of other nations; tests revealed Americans from all walks of life to be shockingly ignorant of the political, economic, and social forces that shape our interdependent world.

In examinations administered by the Educational Testing Service, for example, college students were shown to be lacking in understanding such realities of international life as: the relationship of the U.S. economy to the Organization of Petroleum Exporting Countries (OPEC); the causes of inadequate nutrition as a global problem; the comparative world membership of Islam and Christianity; the current patterns of world birth rates and death rates; the reasons for the lack of substantial progress toward world peace during the twentieth century; the significance of nationalism as a political force; or the meaning of sovereignty.

The realities of today's world make it essential that there be a strong international dimension to our educational system from grade school through graduate school. Jet travel has put us only a few hours from any point on the globe. Television satellite transmissions bring acts of terrorism instantaneously into our living rooms. Indeed, the international perspective of many of our citizens is distorted by the constant flow of news about international violence. The economic, cultural, and political events that constitute international relations are submerged by more sensational news. Yet our long-term survival depends on ability to live in the absence of war, not in its presence.

While the United States and other advanced industrialized countries reap the benefits of modern technology, some 800 million people in the Third World, according to the World Bank, currently live at levels that can only be described as abject poverty. Conversely, technology transfer is creating new economic competition in the developing countries. We only need look at our stores and homes to see evidence of the development of Korea, Hong Kong, Taiwan, Singapore, and other Pacific Rim nations. World problems such as strained trade relations, dwindling resources, overpopulation, hunger, pollution, energy, poverty, lack of adequate communication, inflation, and war all require international solutions.

Our lack of knowledge about other cultures can seriously undermine the nation's foreign policy. Americans are prone to assume—quite erroneously—that our economy and our technology are the envy of the rest of the world and that if underdeveloped countries would only follow the U.S. example, they would discover the secrets of economic progress. Yet only a short time ago in Iran, that assumption was perceived to be directly counter to the basic tenets of the Moslem religion and Iranian culture, and it ripped American policy to shreds.

How many U.S. college graduates since World War II were ever exposed to courses dealing with Islamic cultures? How many Americans today understand the religious roots of the war between Iran and Iraq? How many of us had even a casual knowledge about Southeast Asia before the early 1960s? Or about Korea before 1950? Or, for that matter, about Japan before 1941? Yet in our time Americans have fought three wars in the Pacific basin with little or no grasp of the enemy's history, language, religious beliefs, or culture.

Strengthening International Education

The Commission believes that today's international environment confronts U.S. educators with a threefold challenge:

First, to provide students with an international perspective that reflects the world as it is today in realistic social, political, cultural, and economic terms;

Second, to provide students with international communications skills which will enable them to think, behave, and work effectively in a world of rapid change;

Third, to assist, through research, technical assistance, study, and international service programs, in the resolution of international problems with the same commitment that educational institutions now address domestic issues.

In the Commission's judgment, a critical leadership responsibility for sensitizing Americans and their elected state and national officials to the urgent tasks ahead in the area of international education rests with faculty members and administrators in state colleges and universities. These institutions are regionally based, with roots in every corner of the land. Many of them have already demonstrated extraordinary capabilities in developing outstanding international programs; virtually every state has at least one such institution with a history of overseas ties and commitments, experiences that should be shared across states or regions.

These prototype international programs gauge the extent to which a campus has developed a global perspective, not only in the humanities and social sciences, but also in the total institutional curriculum. They offer an opportunity to encourage the expansion of foreign language and undergraduate area studies programs, not just for social science majors, but also for students in business, engineering, the health professions, and other preprofessional fields. Their guiding premise should be that all students in the university should have a chance to develop an understanding of other cultures, non-Western as well as Western.

Most important for state colleges and universities, which graduate over 50 percent of the teachers annually certified in the United States, is the need to concentrate on improving international education programs for future teachers in the nation's public schools. Some studies brought to the Commission's attention disclose that many social studies teachers today are ill-informed regarding world affairs. In overcoming this "teacher parochialism" in the international area, state colleges and universities must not overlook the imperative to provide opportunities for international experiences for low-income students.

Every scholar who has studied the international education field emphasizes the importance of the institutional mission statement in framing a campus "world outlook." The four Commission-sponsored regional seminars in March and April 1986 urged that the development of such a statement should involve trustees, administrators, faculty members, and professional advisors from other colleges, as well as from abroad. A well-conceived mission statement, in the Commission's opinion, provides a particularly strong incentive to implement international programs in various professional fields, as well as in the liberal arts.

International Education and U.S. Foreign Policy

At the federal level, the Commission believes that the support of education for international understanding should be a fundamental, ongoing component of U.S. foreign policy, and that initiatives in support of international education should be undertaken on four fronts:

First, that state colleges and universities lead the academic community in renewing and strengthening higher education's ties with the Peace Corps, which were so strong in the 1960s and early 1970s, but which have languished in recent years. One possibility might be a compact in which public postsecondary institutions would agree over a long period of time to link Peace Corps service with academic programs for credit and to support Peace Corps recruiting in fields such as teaching and community development. State colleges and universities would also continue to serve as training sites for Peace Corps Volunteers recruited for service overseas.

Second, that state colleges and universities develop internationally oriented courses of study adapted to the special educational needs of business, industrial, professional, and military personnel scheduled for work abroad, particularly emphasizing language and area studies and courses in intercultural understanding.

Third, that Congress establish a national foundation or trust for international education, both undergraduate and graduate, along the lines of the National Science Foundation and the National Endowments for the Arts and Humanities—a partnership effort involving the academic, industrial, and governmental communities.

Fourth, that Congress authorize a long-term student exchange program designed to bring vastly increased numbers of Third World students to study in the United States and to provide American students with the opportunity to study abroad.

This concept is rooted in the conviction that faculty and student exchange programs constitute vital elements in America's continuing role as an international leader. It also recognizes that, given the financial strictures under which the states will be operating for the foreseeable future, international education must be pursued as a direct, continuing responsibility of the federal government. The proposal is predicated on the assumption that our country would be far wiser and more prudent to export education today than run the risk of importing revolution tomorrow.

6.

A Word to State Colleges and Universities

Tacit acceptance of old assumptions about higher education leads to hardening of institutional arteries. The world of this century has changed profoundly and rapidly. It is to that changed world that higher education must respond. Hardened arteries can only inhibit an institution's capacity to respond.

Preventive measures must be taken. For this reason, the Commission calls for bold steps—steps sufficiently bold and large that our imaginations and resolve will be stretched to limits heretofore, perhaps, unthinkable. We call for a state-by-state effort comparable to that of the Marshall Plan of the 1940s and 1950s. Such an achievement will entail a combined and concerted undertaking by higher education leaders and the makers of public policy.

The Commission's thinking has led it time and time again to repeat the proposition that all education is an investment in people. Evidence grows that the return on that investment is real and substantial. We believe that the call must now be for a dramatically increased investment at the level of higher education. Educational practices and public policies must work together toward increasing the investment and making its dividends widely available.

Old assumptions that impede this effort must be either rejected or modified. Assuming that higher education will focus principally on "traditional" students; assuming that modern technology will have little impact on modes of teaching and learning; assuming that state colleges and universities will and should return to a condition of "laissez-faire" autonomy; or assuming that it will be impossible to find the resources to respond to these new challenges could halt the effort even before it is attempted.

Academic Quality

Perhaps no concern about higher education has attracted more attention than the quality of undergraduate education. Most frequently the concern is expressed in terms of deficiencies exhibited by many college graduates in their communication skills, their ability to solve quantitative problems, their knowledge about the world around them, and their competence as critical thinkers.

For example, the three recent national studies by the National Endowment for the Humanities (NEH), the National Institute of Education (NIE), and the Association of American Colleges (AAC) collectively constitute a most serious indictment of U.S. higher education and, indeed, of the entire academic profession. Thus:

"Evidence of devaluation in college curriculums is everywhere. The business community complains of difficulty in recruiting literate college graduates. Remedial programs, designed to compensate for lack of skill in using the English language, abound in the colleges and in the corporate world. Writing as an undergraduate experience, as an exploration of both communication and style, is widely neglected." (AAC)

"The bachelor's degree has lost its potential to foster the shared values and knowledge that bind us together as a society." (NIE)

"A student can now obtain a bachelor's degree from 75 percent of all U.S. campuses without studying European history [and] from 72 percent without studying American literature or history." (NEH)

More recently, three other agencies—the Carnegie Task Force on Teaching as a Profession, the Education Commission of the States (ECS), and the National Governors' Association (NGA)—issued major reports on quality in undergraduate education and the need for dramatic structural changes in policies and practices in the field of teacher education—a professional area of particular concern to state colleges and universities. ECS, in its report, found that "too many students are entering college without the knowledge, skills and attitudes necessary for success in college, a gap [that] will inevitably widen as the nation changes its expectations about what people should know."

Public colleges and universities should respond to these concerns by agreeing on and adopting a set of minimum academic skills and levels of proficiency that all students should attain, preferably by the end of the sophomore year. This should be done on the basis of faculty recommendations and administered in a way that will assure the public that the necessary skills expected from a college education are, indeed, being achieved. Students should be required to match or exceed these threshold requirements, which would provide a basic accountability and a standard upon which individual institutions can build. Each college and university should further specify clearly not only the skills but also the means by which it will facilitate their acquisition by every student before a bachelor's degree is awarded.

Recipients of baccalaureate degrees should have obtained knowledge and experiences that equip them a with sense of competence, relevance, and pertinence for the future. Not only must they function well in a multilingual, technological, global society, but they must also contribute to its advancement and quality. It would be tragic if America's colleges allowed baccalaureate graduates to be monolingual in that global society; to be technologically naive in an age demanding technical skills and sophisticated understandings; or to be uninitiated to the "real-life" worlds of work and of social responsibility.

The dimensions of this undertaking are only gradually being realized:

Study of foreign language and culture should become standard, and over the next fifteen years, state colleges and universities should ensure that all degree recipients master a language other than their native tongue.

Graduates should understand how to use science and technology sufficiently to contribute knowledgeably to public decisions.

Hands-on experiences and internships should expand students' knowledge about the work place and instill a commitment to the public good. At the same time, higher education must continue to increase students' competence and skills; to develop their talent and a love of learning; and to transmit an understanding and appreciation of their own and other cultures.

Faculty Vitality and Excellence in College Teaching

Faculty vitality and excellence in college teaching go hand in hand. Both are characterized by enthusiasm for the subject taught and delight in seeing evidence of student learning. Both are characterized by persistent curiosity about one's discipline and those of others. Both are characterized by an eagerness in encountering new ideas and new patterns of thought. Both are evidenced by energetic response to the challenge of instructing students who are diverse in their educational, ethnic, and cultural backgrounds.

Dynamism of an institution and the quality of its functioning are determined foremost by the interaction between its faculty and students and among students themselves. Searching for strategies to strengthen that interaction should continue to be a matter of highest priority. There will be, as a consequence, matters of both institutional and public policy that will require special attention of educational and public leaders.

Among these are: a faculty reward system that gives full recognition to outstanding teaching; opportunities to be engaged in and to involve students in research, and scholarly or other creative activity; and support for sabbatical leaves, faculty exchanges, and special provisions for gaining new knowledge and developing new academic skills.

The Commission recommends that state fiscal and institutional policies be adopted or modified to ensure that faculty vitality and excellence in teaching are maintained and enhanced.

Leadership and Its Newer Dimensions

In recent years higher education institutions have been subjected to increasing pressures stemming from developments such as the decline in high school populations and subsequent college enrollments, changing student interests, and reduced state and federal resources. These pressures have prodded institutions to focus more of their attention on fiscal matters. In response they have turned to corporate models of strategic planning and management. A number of helpful insights have been gained from this perspective, but there is mounting evidence that the corporate perspective has limited applicability to education.

Because business has *profit* as its bottom-line, a business's effectiveness is largely controlled by its competitive edge. The bottom-line outcome of education is improving students' competencies, knowledge and skills. Strengthening an institution's educational effectiveness, then, is to be found in its *cooperative* dimension. When an educational institution sees itself as competing for students and resources, it is hindered in developing productive consortia, sharing instructional strategies, and mounting joint research ventures. By virtue of drawing support from the same "pie" of state resources, state colleges and universities have a special mandate to be assertive and responsive in exploring the benefits of cooperation within and among their campuses.

Qualities of creative leadership in the past have been, to a large degree, geared to a frontier spirit. Not all, but much of the educational frontier has been explored and structured. America has become a highly interactive community. Thus the new dimensions of leadership will be measured in terms of cooperative endeavors.

The Commission emphasizes the compelling need for such endeavors because the educational task facing the nation looms large. Support for the effort will be encouraged by discovery of cooperative uses of existing resources, as well as the search for new resources. Cooperation—not competition: this is the new challenge for leadership in higher education.

Afterword

On September 17, 1987, the United States will observe the 200th anniversary of its Constitution. As we did on July 4, 1976, in celebration of the nation's bicentennial, and again on July 4, 1986, in saluting the Statue of Liberty on her 100th birthday, we the American people will once again count our blessings.

The Commission believes that all Americans will be able to share those blessings fully and fairly only when our society begins to reach the outer limits of its national potential—a dramatic potential that augurs well for our country's stature as a leader in the community of nations.

While we have taken giant steps toward fulfillment of that goal since World War II, much remains to be achieved, with storm clouds threatening to diminish or forestall our accomplishments. We need only to be aware of the growing American underclass and the vast numbers of disconnected and disaffected youth who daily turn their backs on school, to sense what these clouds portend.

The key element in reaching our national potential, in the Commission's judgment, is a public higher education system that offers everyone a chance to go to college. It is the Commission's conviction that the state colleges and universities are the gateways that make broader access to educational opportunity possible. Dedicated principally, as they are, to undergraduate instruction that rests on a solid foundation of general and professional education, and awarding, as they do, more than 30 percent of all bachelor's degrees, their current and future role is indispensable to the accomplishment of broad national educational objectives. Indeed, without the full support and cooperation of the state colleges and universities, it would be impossible for the public schools to effect the basic reforms called for by the National Commission on Excellence in Education in its Report, A *Nation at Risk*, issued in the spring of 1983. As the American Association of State Colleges and Universities said in its policy statement, AASCU *and the Nation's Schools,* adopted in November 1983, the ``alumni of 'the colleges of the forgotten Americans' have [as teachers] touched the lives of children in virtually every school district in the land.''

Education is basic to every facet of our national life. This Report emphasizes that many, many more Americans need the benefit of the knowledge and skills that a college education can provide. The Commission is persuaded that, unless educational leaders and public policy makers join in a major, new, state-by-state effort to expand educational opportunity, the vitality of our nation will suffer, and our ability to aid in bringing greater stability to the world will disintegrate.

For the United States to shrink from this challenge would be unforgivable.

Those who could not forgive would be those whom we chose, tragically, in the closing years of the twentieth century, not to educate to their fullest potential.

As we prepare to celebrate the beginning of our Constitution's third century, state colleges and universities must squarely face the imperatives of their renewed trusteeship. For they are stewards of the American dream.

Appendices

A

National Commission on the Role and Future of State Colleges and Universities

Chair

Terrel H. Bell, Professor of Educational Administration, University of Utah

Vice Chair, Northeastern Region

Alice Chandler, President, State University College at New Paltz, New York

Vice Chair, Southeastern Region

E. K. Fretwell Jr., Chancellor, University of North Carolina at Charlotte

Vice Chair, Midwestern Region

John Porter, President, Eastern Michigan University

Vice Chair, Western Region

W. Ann Reynolds, Chancellor, California State University

Commissioners

Alexander Astin, Director, Higher Education Research Institute, University of California, Los Angeles

William Oliver Baker, Chairman of the Board (Retired), AT&T-Bell Laboratories

Alison Bernstein, Program Officer, The Ford Foundation

Shirley Browning, Professor of Economics, University of North Carolina at Asheville

Mary Clark, Professor of Biology, San Diego State University, California

The Honorable William Clinton, Governor, State of Arkansas

Ruth Clusen, Regent, University of Wisconsin System

The Honorable Wilhelmina Delco, Representative, Texas State Legislature

Mary Futrell, President, National Education Association

James Gilbert, President, East Stroudsburg University of Pennsylvania

Rob Patterson, former President, Associated Student Government, Southwest Texas State University

Nathan Quinones, Chancellor, New York City Board of Education

Albert Shanker, President, American Federation of Teachers

Hoke Smith, President, Towson State University, Maryland

David Strand, Vice President and Provost, Illinois State University

W. Carl Wimberly, Vice Chancellor, University of Wisconsin-La Crosse

William Winter, Partner, Watkins, Ludlam & Stennis, former Governor, State of Mississippi

B

Summary of Conclusions and Recommendations by Chapter

A Word to the American People

1. Nothing short of a creative state-by-state effort to strengthen education at all levels, comparable to the Marshall Plan in scope, cost, and dedication, can ensure the preservation of our democratic legacy for the twenty-first century.
2. In the judgment of the Commission, the dimensions of such a Project require that:
   - At least 35 percent of American adults should have a college degree by the year 2001.
   - State colleges and universities must assume the leadership role in producing the one million additional public school teachers required to meet the needs of elementary and secondary education during the next decade.
   - State colleges and universities should direct their academic resources and institutional priorities toward working cooperatively with public schools and community colleges to reduce the high school dropout rate by 50 percent over a ten-year period.

Regarding Higher Education and Democratic Values

1. The Commission believes that ways must be found to manage the excellence/equity equation so that the boundaries of our public higher education system are extended, not limited.
2. The Commission views the low-tuition principle in higher education as an extension of the free public elementary and secondary school system, an extension that becomes all the more necessary as America's technological and social complexity increases.
3. The Commission recommends that, in formulating long-range plans for public higher education, state policy makers strive to keep tuition levels at state colleges and universities as low as possible, and that faculty members, administrators, and trustees at these institutions incorporate a commitment to the "low tuition principle" in policies relating to institutional accessibility.
4. The Commission recommends that state colleges and universities recognize the value of student participation in public and community service activities and make every effort to integrate public and community service into the undergraduate curriculum.

Regarding Educational Opportunity in the United States

1. All individuals in our society who aspire to earn a bachelor's degree must have the opportunity to attempt to fulfill that aspiration.
2. At least 35 percent of American adults should have a college degree by the year 2001.
3. To accept this challenge, the state colleges and universities will have to direct their academic resources and efforts toward working with the public schools and the community colleges to cut the high school dropout rate in half by 1996.
4. This country will need one million new elementary and secondary teachers, educational specialists, and school administrators to be trained and placed over the next ten years. With their historic roots as teacher education institutions, America's state colleges and universities are the sector of higher education with the primary responsibility and capacity for meeting this need.
5. Working in close cooperation with the public schools and teacher organizations, state colleges and universities must (a) ensure that the academic preparation of teachers

meets the highest standards expected by the schools and by the public; (b) attract more talented students, including greater numbers of minority students, into the teaching profession; and (c) work in collaboration with teachers in the classrooms at all levels to solve practical problems of improving their teaching skills, developing better methods of student assessment, developing more effective curricula, and enhancing student motivation for learning.

6. Every faculty member should be held responsible for making a contribution to raising the level and the quality of public education to meet the needs of the next century.

7. Because the crisis in teacher education is national in scope, the Commission recommends that Congress reinstate the student loan forgiveness program for college graduates entering the teaching profession.

8. State colleges and universities should be in the forefront of the movement to develop more effective methods of assessing the educational progress of students.

9. Assessment should be seen primarily as a means of enhancing the effectiveness of educational programs, not just as a means of demonstrating academic quality.

10. The Commission recommends that state college and university faculties: assign high priority to research on pedagogy at all levels; develop coherent plans for determining when, where, and to what extent each student should demonstrate progress toward an agreed-upon set of bachelor's degree-level skills; and, paralleling such measures, design instructional strategies to correct deficiencies and to assist students to achieve at higher levels.

11. Each state must make every effort to maintain the distinctions among institutions and their curricular and instructional programs.

12. Historically black public institutions today must be regarded as playing an expanded role in public postsecondary education. They must be recognized as having the same kind of regional significance in regard to applied research and community service that pertains to any other state college or university.

13. For the foreseeable future, state colleges and universities must plan to provide remedial instruction. Recognizing that the foundation of college persistence and achievement is solid academic preparation in high school, state colleges and universities should make a concentrated effort to reduce the incidence of postsecondary remedial education by becoming more actively and directly involved in the preparation of high school students for college study.

14. More school/college cooperative programs should be developed that not only stimulate the talented, but also guide, enrich, and raise the performance levels of underperforming students. This process ought to include joint meetings of college and high school faculty members and administrators and a sharing of data on student performance.

15. Congress should take steps to provide sufficient funds for student financial assistance to rectify the existing imbalance in the federal financial aid program so that the amount of assistance channeled into grants and work-study would be at least equal to that appropriated for student loans.

Regarding Higher Education and Economic Development

1. When a decision is reached to close a state college or university, such action should be taken only as a last resort—only if the state is certain that its educational investment is being reinvested elsewhere, and only if access to higher education opportunities is not being foreclosed.

2. State governments should examine the role that public higher education can play in regional economic development, including the possible expansion of institutional responsibilities in the areas of research and public service.

3. Higher education institutions, both public and private, can and should help governments and businesses achieve economic development goals through economic research and analysis, technical assistance, research and development, technology transfer, and new business development.

4. Congress should create a national program to enhance the role of colleges and universities in community service and economic development.

5. State colleges and universities should restructure their modes of delivery of instruction and student services to give adult and part-time students full access to undergraduate and graduate programs. Specifically, institutions committed to serving adult learners should build on tested cooperative models: work-study programs, instructional television, instruction at the work place, and faculty-designed, computer-aided instruction.

6. Access to continuing education programs should be provided in all regions of the states, to give working people the chance to pursue job advancement while fulfilling their civic and family responsibilities.

7. The federal government should extend financial aid on a full-parity basis to part-time and adult students.

8. Research programs at state colleges and universities should continue to be developed, not only to meet the increasing needs of business and industry, but also to enhance state and regional information resources and to improve the quality of life.

Regarding American Higher Education in an Interdependent World

1. The Commission believes that today's international environment confronts U.S. educators with a threefold challenge:

   ■ First, to provide students with an international perspective that reflects the world as it is today in realistic social, political, cultural, and economic terms;

   ■ Second, to provide students with international communications skills that will enable them to think, behave, and work effectively in a world of rapid change;

   ■ Third, to assist, through research, technical assistance, study, and international service programs, in the resolution of international problems with the same commitment that educational institutions now address domestic issues.

2. A critical leadership responsibility for sensitizing Americans and their elected state and national officials to the urgent tasks ahead in the area of international education rests with faculty members and administrators in state colleges and universities.

3. State colleges and universities, which graduate over 50 percent of the teachers annually certified in the United States, need to concentrate on improving international education programs for future teachers in the nation's public schools.

4. Every scholar who has studied the international education field emphasizes the importance of the institutional mission statement in framing a campus "world outlook." The development of such a statement should involve trustees, administrators, faculty members, and professional advisors from other colleges, as well as from abroad. A well-conceived mission statement, in the Commission's opinion, provides a particularly strong incentive to implement international programs in various professional fields, as well as in the liberal arts.

5. The support of education for international understanding should be a fundamental, ongoing component of U.S. foreign policy, and federal initiatives in support of international education should be undertaken on four fronts:

   ■ First, state colleges and universities should lead the academic community in renewing and strengthening higher education's ties with the Peace Corps.

   ■ Second, state colleges and universities should develop internationally oriented courses of study adapted to the special educational needs of business, industrial, professional, and military personnel scheduled for work abroad, particularly emphasizing language and area studies and courses in intercultural understanding.

   ■ Third, Congress should establish a national foundation or trust for international education, both undergraduate and graduate, along the lines of the National Science Foundation and the National Endowments for the Arts and Humanities—a partnership effort involving the academic, industrial, and governmental communities.

   ■ Fourth, Congress should authorize a long-term student exchange program designed to bring vastly increased numbers of Third World students to study in the United States and to provide American students with the opportunity to study abroad.

A Word to State Colleges and Universities

1. Public colleges and universities should agree on and adopt a set of minimum academic skills and levels of proficiency that all students should attain, preferably by the end of the sophomore year. This should be done on the basis of faculty recommendations and administered in such a way that the public will be assured that the necessary skills expected from a college education are, indeed, being achieved. Students should be required to match or exceed these threshold requirements, which would provide accountability and a standard upon which individual institutions can build. Each college and university should further specify clearly not only the skills but also the means by which it will facilitate their acquisition by every student before a bachelor's degree is awarded.

2. Study of foreign language and culture should become standard, and over the next fifteen years, state colleges and universities should ensure that all degree recipients master a language other than their native tongue.

3. State college and university graduates should understand how to use science and technology sufficiently to contribute knowledgeably to public decisions.

4. State college and university graduates should have the opportunity for hands-on experiences and internships that both expand knowledge about the work place and instill a commitment to the public good.

5. The Commission recommends that state fiscal and institutional policies be adopted or modified to ensure that faculty vitality and excellence in teaching are maintained and enhanced.

6. State colleges and universities should be assertive and responsive in exploring the benefits of cooperation within and among their campuses, including the cooperative utilization of existing resources to further the goals of public higher education in the years ahead.

C

Background of the Report

Creation of the National Commission on the Role and Future of State Colleges and Universities was authorized by the Board of Directors of the American Association of State Colleges and Universities (AASCU) in January 1985.

Their decision was stimulated principally by the facts that: (1) AASCU was about to begin its twenty-fifth year of existence; and (2) fifteen years had elapsed since an earlier commission, chaired by the late U.S. Senator Wayne Morse, had made its report. During that time, many significant changes and developments occurred in higher education generally, and in particular among the nation's 405 state colleges and universities, 372 of which hold membership in AASCU. Their role and future in American higher education needed, in the Board's view, new, intensive examination.

Terrel H. Bell, the former U.S. Secretary of Education, agreed to accept the responsibility of chairing the Commission. Having done so, he proceeded to invite a group of individuals who were broadly representative of higher education and the community at large to serve with him. Twenty-one persons accepted his invitation.

Serving as principal staff to the Commission were Harold Delaney, executive vice president of AASCU, Helen R. Roberts, director of AASCU's Office of Community Development and Public Service, and Lawrence E. Dennis, special assistant to the president of AASCU. Prior to the first meeting of the Commission, on November 23, 1985, the staff gained the assistance of a panel of Senior Advisors in the development of a tentative list of issues to which the Commission could address itself.

At that meeting, on hearing the charge from Chairman Bell to produce a "brief but hard-hitting, positive report," the Commissioners clarified and agreed on an agenda of issues that were subsequently discussed during a series of four "Regional Seminars." A total of more than 200 individuals responded to both open and special invitations to register and participate in the Seminars, held in Charlotte, North Carolina (March 9-10), Los Angeles, California (March 23-24), Chicago, Illinois (April 13-14), and Boston, Massachusetts (April 27-28). Each Regional Seminar was chaired by a member of the Commission.

Additionally, two or more members of the Commission and of the Senior Advisors panel attended each Seminar.

Full involvement of all registrants was ensured by dividing them into small discussion groups of ten to twelve participants. Each group was asked to discuss, at the first session, what special roles state colleges and universities should play in public higher education in light of major societal trends, and what new initiatives they should be undertaking in the future.

The following day's group discussions were devoted to in-depth consideration of the remaining issues before the Commission. (See listing of Seminar Topics, Appendix D.) In addition to having each session audiotaped, professional members of the AASCU staff served as recorders whose notes formed the basis for the Seminars' summary statements presented by the discussion group chairs in a concluding plenary session. Also at each seminar's concluding session, a Senior Advisor provided an overview of the entire Seminar.

In preparation for the second meeting of the Commission, June 5-7, the Commission staff undertook the following: prepared an overall summary of the topics and ideas discussed and developed at the four Seminars; reviewed pertinent literature and compiled for each Commissioner a looseleaf binder containing background documents on the many issues being addressed; and interviewed each member of the Commission whose schedules had prevented attendance at the Seminars. Utilizing this information, the Commission was asked by Chairman Bell to develop, during the course of its two full days of discussion, clear guidance to the staff on the content and tone of the final report. Also attending this meeting were the majority of the Senior Advisors, who were an invaluable resource to the Commission.

Three drafts of the report were prepared. An initial draft was circulated to the Commissioners for their comments and recommendations for change in mid-July, 1986. On the basis of the responses to the first draft, the staff prepared the second draft, which was reviewed by the Commission at its third meeting on August 24, 1986, following which the final draft was written. All Commissioners subsequently concurred with the substance of the Report and its recommendations.

D
Commission Staff

Executive Director
Harold Delaney, Executive Vice President, AASCU
Associate Directors
Lawrence E. Dennis, Special Assistant to the President, AASCU
Helen Roberts, Director, Office of Community Development and Public Service, AASCU
Staff Assistant
Beverly Lighty

Senior Advisors

Kent Alm, Senior Consultant, North Dakota State Legislature
Robert Birnbaum, Professor of Higher Education, Teachers College, Columbia University, New York
Howard Bowen, Professor of Education, The Claremont Graduate School, California
Milton Byrd, President, Charter College, Alaska
Fred Harcleroad, Professor Emeritus, Higher Education, University of Arizona
John King, Distinguished Visiting Professor, University of South Carolina
Roy Lieuallen, former Chancellor, Oregon State System of Higher Education
John Marvel, former President, Consortium of State Colleges in Colorado
D. Justin McCarthy, President Emeritus, Framingham State College, Massachusetts
Sarah Melendez, Associate Director, Office of Minority Concerns, American Council on Education
James Nickerson, former Director, Servicemembers Opportunity Colleges
Marjorie Wagner, former President, Sonoma State University, California
Albert Whiting, Chancellor Emeritus, North Carolina Central University
Stephen Wright, Vice President Emeritus, The College Entrance Examination Board

AASCU Staff at the Regional Seminars

Christina Bitting, Director, Office of Federal Programs
Libby Costello, Coordinator, Office of Federal Programs
Karen Heger, Director, Membership Services
Evelyn Hively, Director, Academic Affairs Resource Center
Richard Jerue, Vice President for Governmental Relations
Meredith Ludwig, Senior Coordinator, Association Research and Information Resources
William A. Miller, Jr., Consultant, Servicemembers Opportunity Colleges
Richard Novak, Assistant Director, Office of Governmental Relations
Susan Ransdell, Program Associate, Communications Services
Patricia Sullivan, Program Associate, Office of Governmental Relations
Mary Margaret Walker, Director of Public Information
Barbara Zweig, Senior Program Associate, Office of Federal Programs

Production Staff

Joanne L. Erickson, Publications Coordinator
Larry Smith, Designer

E

Summary of Topics Discussed at the Regional Seminars

ISSUE A   What distinctive role should state colleges and universities serve in U.S. higher education, in light of their history and contributions, and given current societal trends? What should be the primary educational missions of state colleges and universities?

ISSUE B   Are there certain general learnings that a college-educated person must have? What should be the proper role of general education in the curriculum of state colleges and universities?

ISSUE C   How can state colleges and universities operate to resolve perceived conflicts among access, equity, and program effectiveness? What public policies help to resolve or to aggravate the conflict? What should be the responsibility of the state colleges and universities for providing remedial instruction?

ISSUE D   What principles should govern states in making adequate appropriations for the support of public higher education? What are the roles and responsibility of the governor and state legislators in advocating public higher education? What should be the role of the student and the state, as well as the federal government in financing public higher education?

ISSUE E   What should be the degree of decentralization/centralization with regard to which functions of the institutions? What is the appropriate balance of the need for flexibility at the institutional level with the need for interinstitutional coordination?

ISSUE F   What can the leaders of state colleges and universities do to further the goals of these institutions? What support mechanisms are needed in order for leadership to operate effectively? What kind of people are needed to fill the president's role, and how can they be identified? What leadership roles are required in the governor, the state legislator, the governing board member, the president, the coordinating board member, the executive officer of the system, the faculty, and other constituencies of these institutions?

ISSUE G   What principles should guide state college and university leaders in developing relationships with business, industry, and other elements of the private sector?

ISSUE H   What new initiatives will state colleges and universities be taking to remain on the cutting edge in the next fifteen years?

F

References

AASCU and the Nation's Schools: An Action Program for Excellence and Opportunity in Education. Washington, D.C.: American Association of State Colleges and Universities, 1984.

A Nation at Risk: The Imperative for Educational Reform. A report to the Nation and the Secretary of Education. Washington, D.C.: National Commission on Excellence in Education, 1983.

A Nation Prepared: Teachers for the 21st Century. The Report of the Task Force on Teaching as a Profession. New York: Carnegie Forum on Education and the Economy, 1986.

Auletta, K. The Underclass. New York: Random House, 1982.

Digest of Education Statistics. Washington, D.C.: Office of Education Research and Improvement, U.S. Department of Education, National Center for Education Statistics, 1981.

Hamburg, David A. Reducing the Casualties of Early Life: A Preventive Orientation. Reprint from the 1985 Annual Report of the Carnegie Corporation of New York.

Harcleroad, Fred F. Colleges and Universities for Change: A Pocket History of Americas' Comprehensive State Colleges and Universities. Washington, D.C.: American Association of State Colleges and Universities, 1985.

Higher Education for American Democracy: A Report of the Presidents' Commission on Higher Education, New York: Harper and Brothers, 1947.

Hodgkinson, Harold L. All One System: Demographics of Education, Kindergarten through Graduate School. Washington D.C.: 1985. The Institute for Educational Leadership.

Hodgkinson, Harold L. Guess Who's Coming to College: Your Students in 1990. Washington, D.C.: National Institute of Independent Colleges and Universities, 1983.

Integrity in the College Curriculum: A Report to the Academic Community. The Findings and Recommendations of the Project on Redefining the Meaning and Purpose of Baccalaureate Degrees. Washington, D.C.: Association of American Colleges, 1985.

Involvement in Learning: Realizing the Potential of American Higher Education. Report of the Study Group on the Conditions of Excellence in American Higher Education. Washington, D.C.: National Institute of Education, U.S. Department of Education, 1984.

Issues and Alternatives in the Future of State Colleges and Universities: A Report of the National Commission on the Future of State Colleges and Universities. Washington, D.C.: American Association of State Colleges and Universities, 1971.

Lee, Valerie. Access to Higher Education: The Experience of Blacks, Hispanics and Low Socio-Economic Status Whites. Washington, D.C.: American Council on Education, 1985.

Marks, Joseph L. The Enrollment of Black Students in Higher Education: Can Decline Be Prevented? Atlanta: Southern Regional Education Board, 1985.

Minorities in Higher Education. Fourth Annual Status Report by the Office of Minority Concerns. Washington, D.C.: American Council on Education, 1985.

Reconnecting Youth: The Next Stage of Reform. A Report from the Business Advisory Commission. Denver: Education Commission of the States, 1985.

The Condition of Education. National Center for Education Statistics. Washington, D.C.: Office of Educational Research and Improvement, U.S. Department of Education, 1985.

The Higher Education—Economic Development Connection: Emerging Roles for Public Colleges and Universities in a Changing Economy. Washington, D.C.: American Association of State Colleges and Universities, 1986.

The Status of Children, Youth, and Families, 1979. Washington, D.C.: U.S. Department of Health and Human Services, Office of Human Development Services, Administration for Children, Youth and Families, 1980.

Time for Results: The Governors' 1991 Report on Education. Washington, D.C.: National Governors' Association, 1986.

To Reclaim a Legacy. Washington, D.C.: The National Endowment for the Humanities, 1984.

Transforming the State Role in Undergraduate Education: Time for a Different View. The Report of the Working Party on Effective State Action to Improve Undergraduate Education. Denver: Education Commission of the States, 1986.

America's State Colleges and Universities

The Report of the National Commission focuses on the more than 400 state colleges and universities whose locations are shown on this map.*

Puerto Rico

Virgin Islands

Guam

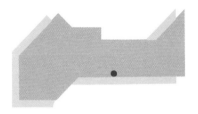

Hawaii

Alaska

---

*In addition, the U.S. public higher education network includes over 900 two-year institutions and nearly 150 state-supported land-grant/research universities.